The Schoolteacher

Pamela McDowell

Weigl

Published by Weigl Educational Publishers Limited
6325 10th Street SE
Calgary, Alberta
T2H 2Z9

Website: www.weigl.ca

Library and Archives Canada Cataloguing in Publication

McDowell, Pamela, author
        Teachers / Pamela McDowell.

(Early Canadians)
Includes index.
ISBN 978-1-77071-892-0 (bound).--ISBN 978-1-77071-893-7 (pbk.)

        1. Teachers--Canada--History--Juvenile literature. 2. Schools--
Canada--History--Juvenile literature. 3. Frontier and pioneer life--
Canada--Juvenile literature. I. Title. II. Series: Early Canadians (Calgary, Alta.)

LA411.M44 2013   j371.00971   C2013-902406-9

Printed in the United States of America in North Mankato, Minnesota
1 2 3 4 5 6 7 8 9 0 17 16 15 14 13

062013
WEP130613

Project Coordinator: Megan Cuthbert
Design: Terry Paulhus

Photograph Credits
Weigl acknowledges Getty Images, Glenbow Museum, and Library and Archives
Canada as the primary image suppliers for this title.

We acknowledge the financial support of the Government of Canada through
the Canada Book Fund for our publishing activities.

CONTENTS

INTRODUCTION

In Canada's early years, there were no formal schools. When settlers moved to an area, they worked hard to build their own homes and farms. Some of the settlers taught their children to read and write, but many did not. Soon after they finished building their homes, people in the community came together to build a schoolhouse and hire a teacher.

Early settlers made their schoolhouses and other buildings from trees found in the area.

A teacher could be a man or a woman. A male teacher was called a schoolmaster. A female teacher was called a schoolmistress. Most teachers lived with a family in the community. Sometimes, the settlers built a small home for the teacher to use. This home was called a **teacherage**.

Most of the teachers in early Canada were men. Women could only work as a teacher if they were unmarried.

LIFE OF A SCHOOLTEACHER

The teacher spent his or her days in the schoolhouse, which was usually a simple log cabin. The floor might be dirt or wood. A few windows would let in enough light to read during lessons. At first, students sat on backless benches with desks made from wooden planks. Later, desks with seats were added. The schoolhouse was heated by a stove that burned wood or coal.

The early schoolhouses had only one room. All of the students sat in the same room, with their desks facing the teacher.

The teacher was responsible for teaching all the students. Sometimes, there were as many as eight grades together at one time. Students were usually seated by grades, with the youngest children at the front. The boys often sat on one side of the room, and the girls sat on the other side.

TEACHING TOOLS

Pioneer teachers had only a few basic tools in the classroom. There were no pencils, markers, maps, or computers like the ones that are used in classrooms today. The teacher had few teaching supplies.

Blackboard

The pioneer teacher's most important tool was the blackboard at the front of the classroom. The blackboard was made of a smooth type of stone. The lessons for each grade were written on a different part of the blackboard.

Slates

Pioneer students did not write their lessons on paper. Instead, students used slates, which were like small blackboards. The smooth, black slate was trimmed with wood so it was easy to hold. The students did **arithmetic** problems and wrote spelling words on their slates. The slate pencils they used scratched and squeaked on the slate. Sometimes, the classroom was very noisy with the sounds of work.

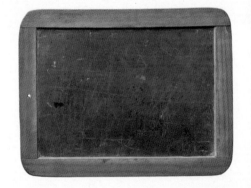

Quills and Ink

It was difficult to practice handwriting on a slate, so the older students used quills and ink. A quill pen was a long feather that had been sharpened at the tip. Students dipped the quill into homemade ink and wrote on paper they had brought from home. Drips, blotches, and smears were common when writing with a quill and ink. Goose and swan feathers made the strongest quill pens.

Readers

Teaching students to read was an important part of the teacher's job, but there were few books in the classroom. At first, students read from the Bible. Later, textbooks were used for learning how to read and spell. These textbooks were called readers.

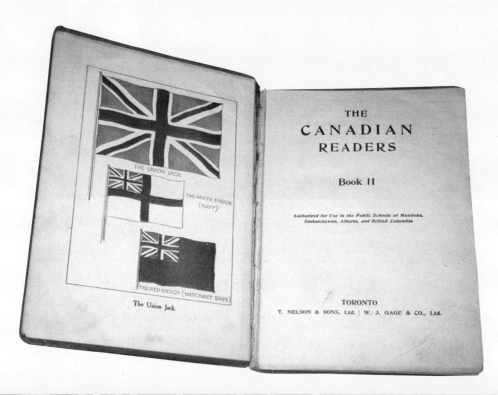

The teacher arrived early each morning to start the fire in the schoolhouse stove. At 8:00 am, the teacher rang the bell to signal the start of school. Students lined up at the door, shortest to tallest. In larger schools that had two doors, the girls lined up at one door, and the boys lined up at the other.

I nside the classroom, students stood beside their desks and said good morning to the teacher. They recited a prayer together or sang a song. The teacher then did a health inspection. All of the students had their ears, hair, hands, nails, neck, and teeth checked to see that they were clean and healthy. Once this was done, lessons began.

LESSONS

T he pioneer teacher only taught three subjects. He or she taught reading, writing, and arithmetic to children from all grade levels. The teacher was very busy working with all different grades in one classroom. Sometimes, older students helped the younger ones with their lessons.

AaBb Cc Dd Ee Ff GgHh Ii Jj KkLl MmNn

Most of the time, students memorized their lessons. Students would complete arithmetic and spelling drills in front of the class. Sometimes, students would use their slates to write down lessons. In later years, teachers taught geography and grammar as maps and books became available.

LUNCH TIME

At 12:00 pm, lessons would stop, and the students and teacher would have lunch. If the weather was good, the students went outside to play. The teacher might have a few minutes to rest before the afternoon lessons.

Lunch was also a good time for students to visit the **outhouse**. Schoolhouses often did not have indoor bathrooms. The teacher rang the bell again to signal the end of lunch and the start of the afternoon lessons.

DISCIPLINE

A teacher had to be very strict to keep students focussed on their lessons. Sometimes, older boys played pranks on other students. They tipped desks or threw firecrackers into the wood stove. These students were punished by the teacher. He or she would hit the students across the hands with a tree branch or leather strap.

Students were also punished for falling asleep or arriving to school late. Their punishment might be to write **lines** or stand in a corner. If the teacher wrote a note home, the student would be punished by his or her parents as well.

The school day ended at 4:00 pm. One or two students stayed behind to help the teacher prepare for the next school day. Students would sweep and clean the classroom. They would also bring in a fresh bucket of water for drinking and washing hands.

The stove was the only source of heat in the schoolhouse. There needed to be enough wood to keep a fire burning throughout the day.

The teacher would fetch coal or wood for the stove and clean the chimney. Sometimes, the teacher also chopped and stacked the school's firewood.

The teacher planned many special events for students during the year. Students took part in a spelling bee each week. They stood at the front of the class and took turns spelling words the teacher read to them. A student sat down when he or she misspelled a word. The last student standing at the front of the classroom was the winner.

The teacher also helped students prepare a Christmas **pageant** each year. Students memorized poems, songs, and plays. They also made decorations. Just before Christmas, parents crowded into the schoolhouse to watch the pageant.

TEACHERS TODAY

TEACHERS

A teacher's job has changed a great deal since the pioneer days of early Canada. Today, a class is made up of students who are all in the same grade. Teachers are expected to teach many different subjects in the younger grades, including history and math. Teachers in the older grades can specialize in one or two subjects. Today, teachers can use many different types of equipment in their classrooms, such as computers, televisions, and textbooks.

THEN AND NOW DIAGRAM

DIAGRAM

Teaching in pioneer days was very different from modern times. The diagram on the right compares these differences and similarities. Copy the diagram in your notebook. Try to think of similarities and differences to add to your diagram.

THEN

- called a schoolmaster or schoolmistress
- taught all the students in one classroom
- did a health inspection each day
- lived with a family in the community
- chopped wood for the stove

- can be men or women
- teach lessons in reading, writing, and arithmetic
- punish students who misbehave
- plan special events during the school year
- use textbooks in the classroom

NOW

- teach one class of students at a time
- teach in large schools with many other teachers
- rely on pens, pencils, and computers

GLOSSARY

arithmetic: the addition, subtraction, multiplication, and division of whole numbers

lines: writing the same sentence over and over

outhouse: a small building containing a pit toilet

pageant: a large performance by all of the students

teacherage: a home the community built for the teacher's use

INDEX